Circa 1930 by Harry Wolf.

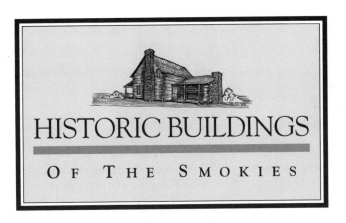

HISTORIC BUILDINGS

O F T H E S M O K I E S

BY
Ed Trout

SIDEBARS BY
Margaret Lynn Brown

For Charles S. Grossman, architect, historian, and "junk man."

EDITED BY: Steve Kemp and Tom Robbins
DESIGNED BY: Christina Watkins
ILLUSTRATED BY: Tony Brown
TYPOGRAPHY AND PRODUCTION BY: TypeWorks
HISTORIC PHOTOGRAPHS: Courtesy National Park Service and Douglas Redding
    (for the Wolf Collection)
COVER PHOTO BY: Richard "Dixie" Atkinson
PROJECT COORDINATION BY: Steve Kemp
EDITORIAL ASSISTANCE BY: Glenn Cardwell, Gene Cox, Lynne Davis, Jo Hoy,
    Kara Rogers, Terry Maddox, and Elden Wanrow

Special thanks to Myrtle Pickel, Elizabeth Powers, and Mark Hannah for
permission to quote from the books of *Reflections of the Pinnacle* and *Cataloochee:
Lost Settlement of the Smokies*.

Printed in the United States of America by EBSCO Media.

This book was printed on Wasau Exact paper which contains 30% recycled
material from post-consumer sources. Great Smoky Mountains Association
advocates the efficient use of recycled and recyclable materials in its publications.

3 4 5 6 7 8 9

ISBN 0-937207-16-0

Library of Congress Catalog Card Number: 95-075130

GREAT SMOKY MOUNTAINS
ASSOCIATION

Great Smoky Mountains Association is a private, nonprofit organization which supports the
educational, scientific, and historical programs of Great Smoky Mountains National Park. Our
publications are an educational service intended to enhance the public's understanding and
enjoyment of the national park. If you would like to know more about our publications,
memberships, guided hikes, and other projects, please contact: Great Smoky Mountains
Association, 115 Park Headquarters Road, Gatlinburg, TN 37738 (865) 436-7318 or visit
www.SmokiesStore.org

CONTENTS

A SENSE OF PLACE

MOUNTAIN HOMES

BARNS & OTHER OUTBUILDINGS

PRESERVING THE HARVEST

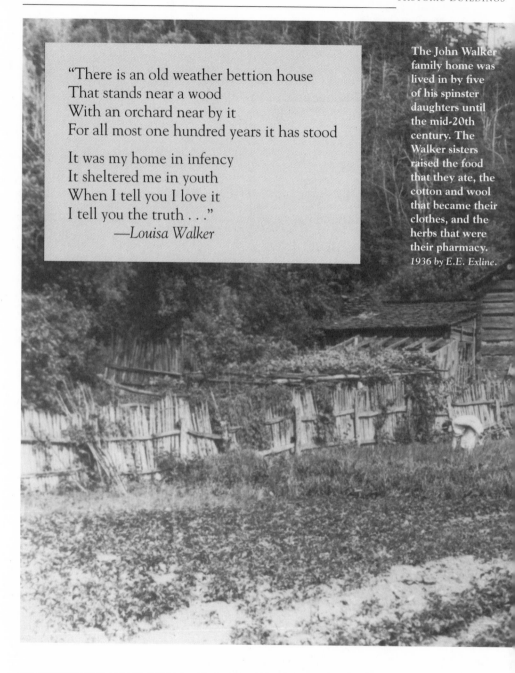

"There is an old weather bettion house
That stands near a wood
With an orchard near by it
For all most one hundred years it has stood

It was my home in infency
It sheltered me in youth
When I tell you I love it
I tell you the truth . . ."
    —*Louisa Walker*

The John Walker family home was lived in by five of his spinster daughters until the mid-20th century. The Walker sisters raised the food that they ate, the cotton and wool that became their clothes, and the herbs that were their pharmacy. *1936 by E.E. Exline.*

A SENSE OF PLACE

LIFE IN THE GREAT SMOKY MOUNTAINS

Great Smoky Mountains National Park is a large place (520,000 acres) lying in two states, and containing the highest mountain range east of the Mississippi River. There are many peaks of 5,000'–6,000' in elevation, surrounded on all sides by valleys, coves, and foothills, and drained by hundreds of small streams. Although old and worn compared to some other mountains, the terrain is steep and rocky at the higher elevations. Razorback ridges are divided by sharp ravines, where "the sun rises at ten and sets at two." Vegetative cover throughout the Smokies consists of several complex coniferous and broadleaf forest types, underlain or bordered by laurel thickets and other brushy growth. Watercourses are fast-moving, clear, cold and flow over rocky beds. Wildlife includes most species that were here before man, and a few that were not. The climate is temperate, and ample rainfall ensures the survival of about any plant or seed that is thrust into the ground. In sum, the environment here is benign, forgiving, and suitable for the growth of plants, animals, and mankind.

Man settled here beyond reach of human memory. Aboriginal people of successive cultural horizons were followed in more recent times by Old World settlers, most of British and Germanic stock. From roughly 1800 to the 1830s, the two cultures coexisted, after which the Indians were forcibly removed to clear the way for an increasing white population. Those pioneers and their descendants remained until they in turn were removed to make way for the national park.

During the century or so that the white population dominated the scene, they progressed from a pioneer and essentially wooden culture, into the machine age. Beginning with a subsistence farming base, they settled in the valleys and coves and up the slopes, clearing away the forest as they went. The natural landscape changed quickly at the lower and middle elevations. Farm buildings, churches, schools, mills, cornfields, orchards, and pastures replaced trees on the flats and foothills. The jangle

of plow harness and beating of the loom supplanted the sounds of wilderness. By the end of the nineteenth century the pioneer period was over, and the agrarian society here was mature. It differed little from rural society anywhere else in eastern America at the time. This, too, was to change quickly. By 1900 the machine age was here. The steam-powered commercial logging industry, financed by northern capital, probed and pierced, and cut and sawed most of the higher forest regions. By the 1920s the first pioneer would never have recognized the Smokies. The land was different. What once was forest was now often blackened and gullied by fires and erosion. The people were different, their old self-sufficiency now dying fast, the lure of cash wages too much to resist.

The twentieth century was here; and then so was the national park. There long had been dreamers, those who knew that they could return this worn out and trampled place to its once-wild state. A stupendous effort was made, and by about 1930 it was done. The land was protected and the wilderness

Progress . . . a board and batten framed addition to the old log homeplace. The black walnut trees in the yard furnished dyes for cloth and attracted squirrels which could be shot from the porch. *Harry Wolf.*

9

encouraged to reclaim its turf. Once again the Smokies became sanctuary to untamed things.

Yet there were a few who insisted that all traces of the human past should not disappear. They knew that there were probably more people doing things in the "old way" here than anywhere else in the East. Those few preservationists persisted and prevailed, so that today some remnants of the cultural past survive. Those bits and pieces, our subject here, are the historic buildings of the Smokies. Through the years they have grown ever more popular and valuable.

THE ARCHITECTURAL POTLUCK

This national park is blessed to have, or to have had, examples of nearly every kind of log domestic and public structure used within the context of eastern rural America. A few highly specialized types did not appear here, such as the semi-subterranean log icehouses of the Virginia mountains. But most did. The end of the log era came in about 1900, as commercial logging and sawmills made lumber easily available for framed structures. Log buildings put up after that time seem to have been the product of extreme and unusual hardship cases, quaint accommodations for the growing tourist trade, or nostalgic novelties. Log buildings from the very earliest days of settlement (1830 or earlier) are extremely rare. However, some of them were described in surveys made in the 1930s before they collapsed. Some of those you see today were in use when their owners moved out of the park. Others were standing abandoned because their owners had progressed to framed buildings. A few were rescued as the green waves of new forest washed up the hillsides. The result is a random table of leftovers, what remains after fate munched its way through the local architecture, as it inevitably does.

IT STARTED WITH AN AX

The log cabin is one of those instantly recognized symbols of the American pioneer era. It ranks up there with apple pie, the flag, and the NFL as a molecule in the national bone and flesh. The average person may not have much technical knowledge of log buildings, but he likes to be around them, to wander through them, to touch them and smell their aged wood. To some, the log building is a piece of family history, something he imagines that his ancestors lived in, whether they really did or not. To someone of purely urban background, the log building is perhaps assimilated into his cultural subconscious as one of the requirements of being "American." This devotion to log buildings is easy to understand. They were found in some form in practically every frontier sector of the East, and in many of the forested areas of the West. Yet they were not the first type of buildings in European America. The Spanish in Florida, for many decades after Columbus, built with mud and sticks, and used coquina stone for large construction. In the Southwest, adobe became their material of choice. The English at Jamestown also used sticks and mud, then brick or lumber, without ever going through a log phase at all. The French in Canada relied, among other things, on the old post and beam. So where do the logs come in? With the Finns and Swedes in Delaware in the mid-1600s. In spite of variations that came later, and debate over their ethnic links, most researchers agree that the simple concept of laying one log on top of another, in eastern America, fanned out from then and there.

From possibly 1700 or so on, log building was adopted by most pioneer groups as they pushed westward from the coastal settlements into the frontier. It became so all-pervading for good reasons. It has been said jokingly, but with a good bit of truth, that in the virgin eastern forest, a squirrel could travel from Maine to Florida without ever touching the ground. Thus, in such a heavily wooded region, building with logs was the quickest and most obvious way to get one's family under some kind of shelter. For the most primitive kind of building, the only tool needed was an ax. To build and furnish a much nicer home, the necessary tools would fit into one large suitcase.

❧ Log & Stone

Henry Davis doesn't harbor fond memories of building a log cabin—it was just plain hard work. Of course, he was only eight years old when he helped his father, John Davis, build the Davis/ Queen house now at the Oconaluftee Mountain Farm Museum. (Queen was a later owner.)

As Henry remembered, his father wanted to live in the mountains so he could free range his hogs and cattle. In 1885, John moved to Indian Creek, where he married a local girl and eventually saved the money to purchase land. The young family then built their new home over a two year period around 1900. After neighbors helped raise the walls, son Henry recalled, "it stood there at least a year, part of it, before it was ever covered."

Once he could provide his family shelter, John moved everyone to the site, but the work was far from finished. That winter "we had to build a fence and clear land to make a crop and work on the house all at the same time more or less," said Henry. "And Daddy put me and my brother . . . carrying locust stakes right up the hill. I was eight and my brother was just a little over four. And I mean those stakes [were] nine feet long locust stakes."

Most of the time the two brothers didn't grumble about the work. Because they were children, though, they sometimes made a game out of a job or just became distracted by other activities. "And

he would fret, you know," Henry recalled, "but well now you couldn't blame him!"

In addition to dragging the locust tree logs, Henry piled the brush and scrap timber and burned it. "When that was through

it was March," Henry said.

The last job Henry remembered was bringing an arched rock from the mouth of the branch for the chimney. He drove the family's aged steer "up that old steep snakin' road" with a sled. The rock, which measured about 12″ by 12″ by 5′ didn't fit completely on the sled and so the back end had to be dragged. "That steer just go 'bout length of himself and stop." Henry recalled.

The magnificent Davis/Queen log house and kitchen. The only log house in the

"It took me all day."

The "pretty heavy rock" Henry carted in 1902 still frames the chimney in the Davis/Queen house near the Oconaluftee Visitor Center.

Smokies with a decorative shingle pattern underneath the eaves.
1960 by Carmen Carter.

MOUNTAIN HOMES

LOG CABINS

Frank Lloyd Wright once said that he could design a house in such a way that it would cause its occupants to get a divorce. The log cabin was not exactly what he had in mind, but it surely came close to the mark. It was the mobile home of its day. Size-wise, the "average" 18′ × 20′ cabin contained only 360 square feet downstairs. Even with a marginally usable sleeping loft, the space increased to only 720 square feet. Compare that to today's "starter home" of 1200 square feet, for young couples with no children, or one or two at most. Into the tiny log house, place the "average" family of two parents, maybe one grandparent, and

Left: a log cabin used by herders or hunters high on Spence Field. Herders were paid by the head to watch other people's livestock during the spring and summer. *Circa 1920. From Randolph Shields collection.*

five to ten children. Shut the doors and windows in the winter with it pouring rain outside, and everyone up and about. It must have been like eating and sleeping with a litter of puppies. This house was hot in summer, drafty in winter, and crowded all year. That is why their occupants spent so much time on the porch, in the yard, or at the barn. It is also why most people aspired to a larger framed house, and upgraded to one as soon as they could manage. Even as early as 1900, and before, photographs document families living in larger, better framed homes, with the old log home standing in the background. Thus, romantic notions of

Right: the Harmon Place at Cane Gap, near Cades Cove, Tennessee. Crops and garden occupy the front yard rather than a lawn. *1936 by C.S. Grossman.*

blissful life in a log cabin properly belong to calendar photos and bluegrass ballads.

The house is the most important part of a mountain farm. It is where the family eats and sleeps, and takes shelter from rain, snow, heat, cold, and other forms of adversity. Without a roof overhead, there is no home. The house (or cabin) was normally the first building to be constructed on a new homestead. Its shape and size were the sum of the family's needs, and the resources available to fill those needs. Resources included raw materials at hand, tools to shape them, people to use the tools, and cash to buy nails and other items that the forest did not provide. The array of different building methods and house configurations in the Smokies demonstrates that people changed

Left: the Bales family dogtrot house was built in stages instead of all at once. Note the separate roofs and different sizes of logs in the two units.

or added onto their homes as they were able to, or as their needs changed. This variety also expresses the differing opinions and attitudes, tastes and skills, of which human brains and hands are capable.

The rectangular single pen was the most common configuration for a home. It could be added onto in several ways as time and circumstances allowed. It was usually $1^1/2$ stories high, meaning that only two or three rounds of wall logs rose above the loft floor before the roof system began. This provided a normal ceiling height downstairs, and enough headroom

Right: a log home on the upper reaches of Roaring Fork Creek. Note the chicken nests in the chimney corner.

upstairs for the kids to sleep and move around. (Full two-story houses appeared occasionally, but were not the norm.) The home had a fireplace with an exterior chimney at one end, a door centered in the front wall, and perhaps a back door aligned with the front one. Window openings were optional at the time of construction, for they could always be sawn out later. However, just as there is no mathematically average human being, there was no mathematically average cabin. Eighteen-by-twenty feet was extremely common, with rectilinear sizes on either side of this, and always in multiples of two feet. Front and rear porches were optional, but were almost a necessity since so many household chores could be done there.

single pen

In addition to the rectangular single pen, there were two other major configurations in the Smokies. They were the "saddlebag" and the "dog-trot," both found elsewhere in the South. The dog-trot could be built as such all at one time, or created later. It consisted of two identical cabins built side-by-side, about 8'–10' apart, with an open breezeway or dog-trot between. All was covered by one continuous roof. This provided a room for cooking and eating on one side, and sleeping and living space on the other. The dog-trot offered sheltered space for working or socializing. Obviously, the dogs made good use of this space, which was cool in summer and relatively warm in winter. The Palmer house in Cataloochee and the Ephraim Bales house on Roaring Fork Motor Nature Trail represent this style very well. The saddlebag house was sort of a reverse of the dog-trot. Instead of two units with a fireplace and chimney at each outer end, the saddlebag consisted of two units so close together that they shared a common chimney. A fireplace in either side of the chimney heated each unit. From a distance this shape apparently reminded one of a pair of saddlebags hanging from the sides of a horse. A liberal imagination is required to make this connection.

saddlebag

dog-trot

The advantage of the saddlebag house was that only one chimney had to be built, and it radiated heat into both units, making the house more thermally efficient. However, it lacked the additional sheltered space of the dog-trot. The Alfred

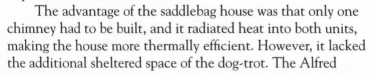

Reagan saddlebag house on Roaring Fork Motor Nature Trail appears to have been built all at once; whereas the Noah "Bud" Ogle house on Cherokee Orchard Road is known to have been built one unit at a time as the family grew. A final configuration among the log houses of the Smokies was either very rare or actually unique. The Henry Whitehead home in Cades Cove began as a very crude cabin, built for Matilda Shields by her brothers. After she married Whitehead, the family built a very nicely done sawn log house directly in front of the old one. The back porch of the later one slightly overhangs the roof of the older one, providing a covered passageway between the two.

A kitchen addition changed the configuration of the house. It was usually a separate structure that stood a few feet away from the house, or perhaps up against it, but whose walls were not actually tied into it. It was normally added at the rear, giving the house an "L" or "T" shape. The kitchen often almost doubled the downstairs living space of early houses, which was good because so much of life centered on food preservation, preparation, and serving. The log house at the Oconaluftee Mountain Farm Museum has a good example of this type of addition. The Elijah Oliver house in Cades Cove offers a little different twist. The kitchen is behind, but lower than, the house; so the two are connected by a set of stairs covered by a roof. At the Walker sisters' place the reverse of the norm occurred. The smaller "kitchen" was the original home, onto which the family built a two-story house. The older edifice then became the kitchen.

ẽ Kitchens

Dora Proffit Williams grew up in a four-room home in Greenbrier. During an oral history interview, she lovingly recalled the contents of the kitchen. "We were proud of our Home Comfort Range," she remembered, "because very few people could afford one." The stove had "warming closets" above the cooking unit and a tank kept filled with water for doing dishes.

Besides the stove, the kitchen held a wood box for the "stove wood" and a "water table" for buckets of spring water. "There was the 'meal gum' which consisted of a large hand-made box in which we kept the flour and meal and a home-made tray. The tray was to make biscuits in," she added. The only other furniture in the room was a homemade corner cupboard and a dining table. "There were no chairs which we left sitting around the table," Williams explained. "When we were called to a meal, we knew to come bringing us a chair."

After the question of configuration was answered, there were several other matters to address. What species of trees to use, or, what was even available for use? To hew, or not to hew? Would purlins, or rafters, support the roof? Would boards, or shingles, cover the house? Was window glass available, and affordable? Would puncheons, or sawn lumber, be used for flooring?

So on it went, choosing from the possibilities. Raising the owner-built home, in a cashless society, with hand tools and handmade components, in a remote rural situation, called for thinking these things out ahead of time.

The forests of the Smokies offered a vast quantity and variety of trees. The species favored for log construction were: Eastern hemlock, the pines, the oaks, American chestnut, and tuliptree. Important qualities were: the shape of the tree trunk, workability under the tools, and resistance to rot and insect attack. The pines, mainly white, pitch, or shortleaf, grew straight and tall with very little taper throughout their length. (Notice the next thousand power poles that you see. They will all be pines.) An even-aged stand of small hemlocks could produce logs with characteristics similar to the pines, although the wood is stringy and aggravating to work. Tall, small diameter oaks, grown in forest conditions that eliminated lower limbs, were occasionally used. Logs of this type were rare, however. Therefore, oak was not a frequent choice in spite of its durability and other qualities.

American chestnut was a favorite for its insect and rot resistance, and its relative softness compared to oak. However, the growth habit of the tree was peculiar. It tapered out widely at the stump; and this tendency was so pronounced in an older tree that the trunk became almost wedge-shaped. Thus, younger, less-tapered trees were preferred. There is one cabin, however, all of whose wall logs were allegedly split out of one large chestnut tree.

The overwhelming choice, hands down, was tuliptree. It is a fairly soft wood, which works easily under sharp tools; yet it has good strength in large dimensions such as logs, posts, and beams. Kept off the ground and dry, tuliptree does not suffer

Like most others, the Walker sisters did much living on the front porch. Their loom, spinning wheel, and other tools of life were there. 1936 by E.E. Exline.

much from rot and insect attack. Best of all, its tall, straight, hardly tapered trunks could be found in large stands, and in almost any desired diameter. Smaller ones, 12″–18″ in diameter, were plentiful, as were the four foot intermediate ones, as used in the Little Greenbrier School building. Split tuliptree floor puncheons 28″–30″ wide were commonly used before sawn lumber was available. The true monster tuliptrees of six–seven foot diameter were simply unmanageable for domestic construction purposes. Overall, it appears that tuliptree was used in 50%–60% of log buildings in the Smokies, all other species combined comprising the remaining portion.

The first step in building a log structure was to cut the trees, and drag the logs to the site with horses, mules, or oxen. If the logs were to be used in the round, Scandinavian-style, then their ends could be notched and the logs laid up without further ado. Sometimes the bark was peeled first, sometimes not. The amount of work that went into the house could depend solely on whether the family was really going to settle down, or was just "trying out" the location. If the logs were to be hewn, then much hard labor lay ahead. Why bother? The reasons given for hewing vary according to whomever you ask. Most well-informed old-timers would agree that hewing reduced the weight of the logs by one-third or more so that they were easier to lift into place. It also removed most or all of the sapwood, which was more prone to rot than the heart, and yielded flat surfaces inside and out so that later the walls could be weatherboarded and papered or paneled. Blind, unreasoning habit seems also to have been a factor. There are quite a few outbuildings whose small poles or logs were hewn, ever so slightly, when there

Hewing could be done while standing or kneeling. Either way, with a 10–12 pound tool, it was backbreaking work. *1926 by Laura Thornborough.*

was no practical need for it. A corncrib, for instance, would never be sealed from ventilation, and its poles were light enough to lift easily. It is as if they were hewn "just a lick," just to make sure that the gods of building were appeased.

The hewing process was simple enough in concept. Chalk-lines were snapped down two sides of a log. An axeman then scored stop-cuts along the sides by chopping into the log with a felling ax at about a forty-five degree angle to the log. After this he used a broadax to slice off the previously-scored sides. By disciplining himself to "hew to the line," he ended up with nice flat faces on either side of the log. Sometimes the top and bottom surfaces were left rounded; and sometimes the log was laid on its side and hewn as before to make it rectangular or square. Since hewing was an absolutely backbreaking job, done with a large, heavy tool, it is no wonder that so often the sides only were hewn, and the bark left on the top and bottom. It should be pointed out here that wall logs were not "adzed," as much modern literature and advertising seem to claim. Also, the badly gashed and pitted logs found in modern log homes have no connection with historic reality. A good scoring and hewing job would leave the log face smooth, with only the faintest of tool marks remaining.

Once they were cut to length and hewn, the logs were notched on the ends and laid up. Notching, or "corner tim-bering" as the academicians call it, was done to lock the four corners of the crib together. There were several basic notch types, and scholars have tried, without much success, to link each to some ethnic group back in the Old World. Each type no doubt represents some person's or group's notion, way back in time, that this notch locked better and shed water better than that notch.

The types used here were: saddle (round), full-V, half-dovetail (chamfer), and square. The full dovetail was not docu-mented at all, anywhere in the Smokies. The saddle and "V" were most often used with round logs or poles. The half-dovetail (chamfer) was by far the most common notch used with hewn logs. The square notch was not very common because it didn't

saddle notch

full-V notch

half-dovetail notch

square notch

lock under compression, and it didn't shed water. That meant that it could be pulled apart by bears, kicked apart by mules in a stall, or would rot. One theory is that the square notch was derived from construction of hasty and temporary British military earthworks, although that may or may not be so. Modern Canadian log construction instructors and builders have invented all kinds of notches that are truly works of art; but they are not to be confused with the simple and adequate techniques of the pioneers.

Laying up the crib was the heaviest and most difficult work. Usually the builder tried to find the best "corner men" in the community to come out and notch the corners as each round was laid. Sometimes in remote situations he had to do the best he could, or go it alone. Whatever the case, the process was always the same. Each log was lifted or skidded on poles to the top of the incomplete wall, the notch laid out and scribed, sawn and chiseled, tried for fit, and rolled into its final resting place. Unless the workman was a real expert, the log had to be rolled over and trimmed a couple of times at least before it fit well. As the wall got higher, the lifting, fitting, and manhandling became increasingly difficult. A green log, 6″ × 12″ by twenty feet long, weighs several hundred pounds. If it falls, it can snap your arm, leg, or neck without ever slowing down.

Once the crib was laid, the roof system was built. There were two basic ways to do it: with purlins and no rafters, or with rafters and lath. Purlins are logs or poles that lie along the long axis of a roof, spaced about two to four feet apart up each slope. Their ends rest on increasingly shorter logs that form the gable ends until the roof peak is reached. True "roof boards" (as the old-timers call them) several feet long can be nailed from purlin to purlin, until the house is covered with only two or three courses of long planks. This was an early form of roof construction, one that eliminated the need for sawn or split boards to close the gables, rows of lath on which to lay shorter shingles, and hundreds of nails. The main disadvantage of this system was that the long boards tended to warp and did not make a very tight roof.

Roof construction with purlins.

Roof construction with rafters.

The other basic roof form consisted of light rafters (either round poles, or hewn or sawn timber) whose bottom ends rested on plate logs atop the walls, and whose top ends were propped together, forming a tent-like frame. Onto these were nailed strips of lath running lengthwise on the roof, and spaced according to the length of shingles to be used. The shingles were then laid onto the lath, each course overlapping by a few inches the one below it. The gables were then closed with split or sawn boards, nailed in place either vertically or horizontally. The advantage of this system was that the materials were lighter in weight and smaller in unit size (rafters, lath, and shingles) than heavy purlins, gable logs and roof planks. However, there were more pieces to make by hand, and they required many times more nails (scarce and expensive in the woods) to attach them. The Walker sisters and Elijah Oliver roofs illustrate the purlin system, although the owners laid rafters, lath and shingles over the original roofs as a later improvement.

After the walls were up and the roof on, it was time to cut the holes in the walls for the windows, doors, and fireplace. With pencil (or chalk or charcoal) in hand, the outline of each was drawn on the wall logs, using a board or string as a guide. Rocks or chunks of wood could be stuck between the logs at the edges of openings to keep the logs from dropping as they were sawn through. If the builder had enough boards and nails (or wooden pegs), he could go ahead and frame the openings at this time. When all was ready, a handsaw could be used between the logs to start a downward cut through the topmost log in the

☾ Building by the "Signs"

"You see'd houses in the mountains where the boards cup up?" asked Birgie Manning, making a curling motion with her hand. "That's when they cured 'em on the new of the moon." Just as many people still plant their gardens by the proper celestial sign indicated on their *Farmer's Almanac*, some Smoky Mountain farmers built their homes by the "signs."

"Boards had to be put on [the house during] the dark of the moon," said Paul Woody, who grew up in Cataloochee. His father always laid the "worm" or outline of a split rail fence in the dark of the moon, otherwise this first rail would rot. "The other rails could be laid any other time," he said. Although he said he didn't believe in "signs" completely, Woody said "to be fair with you I have to go along with a lot of them."

future hole, until a crosscut saw blade could be inserted to do the rest of the job. After the hole was cut, jamb pieces would be nailed or pegged to the ends of the logs on the inside of the openings. Doors were most often made on the spot, of several boards laid side-by-side and tied together with battens (narrow boards) nailed crosswise. Hinges of metal or wood were then attached, and the door hung. Window openings could be closed with wooden shutters, greased paper which is translucent, or glass if available.

Fireplace and chimney units came in three varieties: mud, stick, and stone combinations, all stone, or all brick. The first was definitely the crudest, and was most often used in transitory situations where the family might not intend to stay in the cabin for very long. To build this type, a firebox was laid of stones, as found, using mud as a bedding material. Above the firebox, a chimney was built of small logs or sticks laid in log crib fashion and plastered heavily with mud. As the heat of the fire dried the mud, it gradually fell out in chunks, exposing the sticks underneath. Such chimneys often caught fire and burned the house down. None of these primitive chimneys survive in the Smokies today.

Worn-out wagon wheel tires were often recycled into fireplace lintels. *1936 by C.S. Grossman.*

The most common unit was built entirely of stone, either as found, or with shaped pieces in a few rare cases. As in the stick chimneys, mud was used as a bedding material for the stones. Brick chimneys on log houses were rare, but did exist. The bricks were made on-site, by hand, in wooden molds, and fired (or "burned") on the spot. The Dan Lawson and Henry White-head houses in Cades Cove, and the Jim Hannah cabin in Little Cataloochee have the only surviving ones, and there is no doubt that a brick chimney was an object of status and pride. One of the more interesting little details for "chimney watchers" is construction of the fireplace lintel. A lintel is a building member that spans the top of an opening, be it door, window, fireplace,

❧ Home Improvements

Mountain women, who spent more time indoors than anybody, pressed their husbands for bright and roomy frame houses. For such reasons, Andy Montheith started building his wife a new frame home on the North Carolina side of the Smokies during the 1920s. Before he had time to finish it, however, he embarked on an extended bear hunt.

In his absence, his disappointed spouse tore the shingles off the roof of their old log cabin. This way, the husband was forced to finish the frame house as soon as he returned. He never did finish the chimney, though, and as long as they lived in that house the stove pipe stuck out a hole in the wall.

Even those who stayed in a log homeplace in later years insisted on frame house-style improvements, such as lattice work under the porch. A homestead on Goldmine Branch near Forney Creek added running water, conveyed by gravity down a tube to a trough on the porch. Calvin Welch built a waterwheel that powered electric lights and a woodworking shop. And everyone wanted windows. J.B. Woody re-built a log cabin that had burned down with one improvement: windows. One homeowner on Chambers Creek was so proud of the new glass windows on his box house that he never bothered to wash off the manufacturer's stickers. In a historic photograph, they look like bright decorations in the corner of each pane.

A store-bought window upgrades a log house. By mounting it sideways, only one log had to be cut, thus weakening the wall very little. *1937 by C.S. Grossman.*

etc. Some fireplace lintels here were one large stone laid flat, two stones propped to form an inverted "V," or stones corbelled (stairstepped) out from either side until they met at the top. Others were made of recycled iron wagon wheel tire, either left arched or flattened out. The lintel in the Walker sisters' kitchen fireplace was simply a log that spanned the opening. Amazingly, it served for over a century without burning in two, and is still in place.

The floor of the house was laid on joists that spanned from one wall to its opposing one. Most often the joists were round logs that were halflapped at the ends to fit into the sills, and were slightly hewn on the top side to give a flat seat for the flooring. The flooring was always of puncheons or sawn lumber—assuming the circumstances were past the dirt floor stage. Puncheons were used where sawn lumber and nails were not yet available. The workman would split a short log, in the manner of a hot dog roll, and lay the halves from joist to joist, round side down. The roughly flat upper surfaces would then be dressed with a foot adze or ax until smooth enough to eliminate toe-catching edges and large splinters.

Puncheons lying side-by-side never fit very well, so there were usually substantial cracks between them. Old-timers used to quip that, "You could take the table scraps and feed the chickens through the floor." Since the puncheons rarely seated on the joists just exactly right, and rocked a little bit, a puncheon floor made a peculiar clunking sound as one walked around on it. The cure for drafty cracks and clunking was the sawn lumber floor. Sometimes lumber was available and affordable when the house was built, and sometimes it was added later, often being nailed right on top of the puncheons. The loft floor (or downstairs ceiling) was always of sawn lumber. A puncheon floor would

✄ Granny Holes

Some log houses had tiny, square windows situated near the chimney. These were called "granny holes" because the grandmother of the household spent a lot of her time by the hearth. She would sit on a special low chair and sew or knit as she tended the cooking in the fireplace. The window gave her a little extra light to work by and let her keep track of the comings and goings outside the house.

Cat holes in walls and doors were common in mountain homes. *Circa 1930–35 by Harry Wolf.*

have been extremely heavy to build; and if it failed, it could have crushed the family downstairs.

The loft flooring was laid on poles or hewn joists, which gave the downstairs ceiling the "exposed beam" look that is so popular today. In this type of house, the loft (or upstairs room) never had a ceiling. So, the children sleeping there had the pleasure of staring at the underside of the shingles, and often waking with powdered snow having blown in and drifted all over their bed quilts.

Efforts to tighten the walls against the weather included use of many combinations of materials: mud chinking, mud and rock, mud and bricks, mud and horsehair or straw, mud and wood, exterior battens, interior battens, interior paneling, and wallpaper. Again, the intended length of use of the house determined how far the builder went with this.

Mud chinking depended on a nearby source of red or yellow clay, something not always available in a land where bedrock often lies under a thin layer of loamy topsoil. If used, the clay was mixed with water to a stiff consistency (say, about like peanut butter) and packed into the chinks (cracks) between the logs with the fingers. That is why a correctly restored log house will bear long rows of finger-sized furrows in the chink-

Although it required considerably more work, puncheons could also be made with flat bottoms and laid across the joists as flooring.

ing, rather than a nice smooth steel-trowel finish. In order to provide a more solid base, some small degree of tensile strength, and use less mud, filler material could be placed in the chinks first, and the mud slathered over it. Inevitably, the mud would begin to fall out as it dried and shrank, or be broken up by mice, carpenter bees, or children, until re-chinking became necessary. This was done every few years, or according to need. Battens were often nailed over the chinks, inside or out, or both. Battens could be short and split, like shingles, or sawn and long, like lumber. The better log houses had wide handplaned paneling boards inside, but such finishing was rare.

Finally, there was paper. Commercial wallpaper was used in the Smokies, but mostly in framed houses. Newspapers and magazine pages were glued to the walls with a paste of flour and water. After a few years and several layers of build-up, the thick mass would begin to fall off due to its own weight. It was time, then, for mother and children to pull it all off and start fresh at bare wood.

Interior furnishings could be plentiful or sparse, depending on the family's needs, means, energy, skills, and size. There is plenty of evidence in both directions. Compare the Walker sisters' bewildering array of possessions to those of one poor fellow who moved his family in "three wheelbarrow loads." Furnishings and utensils were not necessarily a measure of wealth or status, particularly in the earlier years of settlement when tables, chairs, benches, beds, etc., were often handmade of materials from the nearby woods. Certain items did have to be purchased, and thus required cash or goods for barter at the store. Kerosene lamps and oil, clocks, mirrors, metal buckets, mattress ticking and such were typical of those. The most important criterion about fur-

§ Air Conditioning

Although mountaineers put chinking or daubing between the logs, cabins were not airtight. "Sometimes the snow would blow in on the bed through the cracks, but it was good for us," wrote Lona Mae Parton Tyson in her memoir, *Reflections of the Pinnacle.* "It kept us healthy and ready to get out and make snowmen and skate on the creek when it was frozen over with ice or track rabbits in the snow. We were hardly ever sick." According to folklorist Michael Ann Williams, some log houses had cracks so large "you could throw a cat through." Because real windows were few, children sometimes created gaps in the daubing to have a place to look out on a gray day.

nishings was that they be functional. If it didn't have a use, it usually wasn't there.

SAWN LOG HOUSES

Perhaps the most unusual, and least-appreciated, house in the park is the Henry Whitehead sawn log house in Cades Cove. Sawn log houses were not unknown, but were extremely rare. Only two were known to exist in the Smokies, and only one survives. It stands both off the beaten path on Forge Creek Road, and on the technological fence between hewn log and sawn framed construction. It is built so well, and its true nature so subtle, that it largely goes unrecognized for what it is. Many visitors have walked all around the outside of it, subconsciously seeing a simple framed house with smooth, wide, horizontal "siding," only to be startled when they eventually notice the notched corners of this log building. This structure is surely what every other log house "wanted to grow up to be."

The advantages of a sawn log house were well worth considering. It made perfect sense, given that all one had to do was to run the logs through the sawmill, instead of laboriously hewing them. The log house required about 30 to 50 percent more timber than the framed house; but if plenty were available on one's own property, so what? The log house required no cash outlay for nails, except for those to install the shingles.

Nor was the log house painted, which eliminated another cash expenditure. The walls are solid and thick (four inches in this case), which provided a measure of insulation not found in the uninsulated framed homes of the day. Finally, there was the sheer weight and strength of the log crib, as opposed to the lightness and *relative* fragility of the balloon frame. In the late 1970s, a small tornado touched down in Cades Cove, picked up a large white pine tree, and dropped it on the Whitehead smokehouse (the small building in the back yard). The roof was crushed, but the log walls were unharmed. The proof is in the puddin', they say.

The wall logs of the Whitehead house have very little taper, and lie perfectly atop one another. Some of them were

A red or yellow clay bank near the house was handy when rechinking time rolled around, which, unfortunately, was every few years since bees, children, mice, and rain made sure that it fell out.
1936 by C.S. Grossman.

❀ All the News Fit to Paste

Lona Mae Parton Tyson, who spent part of her childhood on Copeland Creek, remembered how much work it was to "wallpaper" the house. First the children carried water from the spring to scrub the walls, and "it seemed like it would take a million gallons of water to clean the old house." With the help of their mother, they used "so much flour" to make a paste. "I guess it kept [editor] Bill Montgomery in business using his *Vindicator* paper [on the walls]," Tyson joked. "Then we would lay and read the papers on the wall by lamp light." A historian who studied log cabins in the region found that many people reminisced about playing games by locating words on the walls. The newspaper also made dark cabin interiors brighter. "They looked so clean and white," Tyson emphasized.

The Walker sisters papered their interior walls with magazines, catalogs, and other materials. *1936 by E.E. Exline.*

split in the saw, and one half laid above its mate in the wall. A challenging little pastime is to see how many pairs you can find by matching up opposing knots. There is hardly any chinking in the building, for there was little need, or room, for any. The corners fit as tightly as those of a dovetailed dresser drawer. The telltale vertical marks of the sash saw appear on the flat faces of the exterior wall surfaces. Some remain on the interior surfaces, although many of those were cleaned off with a hand plane. The ceiling joists and trim were also handplaned. Finishing off this fine house is a brick fireplace and chimney. The present unit is a restoration of the original, whose bricks were handmolded and fired on the property.

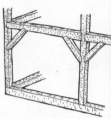

timber framing

Family lore says that this house was the fulfillment of a promise by Whitehead to his bride, Matilda Shields, that he would build her the finest log house in Cades Cove. From the looks of it, he did.

MIXED BUILDINGS

Not everyone who had log buildings and wanted framed ones made the transition all at once. There was usually a gradual changeover as time, money, and convenience allowed one structure after another to be replaced. Even after the transition was complete, the old buildings were often left standing to be used for storage or some other new purpose.

box framing

The alternative to replacement with new construction was "remodeling," to use a latter-day term. Enlarging log structures with framed additions, and concealing the old with new weatherboarding, yielded the "mixed" building. Two of the best examples of mixed houses are the Palmer and Woody homes in Cataloochee. The Palmer house is a dog-trot log house with framed additions, weatherboarding, and interior paneling that conceals the logs. The Woody place is a single-pen log cabin with a framed addition on one end that created a T-shaped house. The logs were covered inside and out to "modernize" the home in about 1910. In Cades Cove, the Tipton-Oliver and Dan Lawson houses illustrate the mixed buildings.

balloon framing

Conservation, frugality, the wisdom of recycling, and sentimentality for "the old homeplace" were always part of the rural mindset. Thus, most farms contained a mixture of buildings well into the twentieth century.

The Proffitt house, near Cosby, Tennessee, is a good example of mixed log and frame construction. *Circa 1930–35 by Harry Wolf.*

FRAMED AND BOXED BUILDINGS

The people of the Smokies, as those elsewhere, did not live in and use log buildings any longer than necessary. They understood perfectly the technical advantages, and the prestige value, of other types of construction. Therefore, from about 1870 to 1900, log building was increasingly abandoned in favor of framed construction. When the national park was being developed in the early 1930s, there were hundreds of framed homes, barns, outbuildings, schools, churches, stores, and mills in use in the Smokies. They were considered at that time to have been "modern" structures, rather than "pioneer" buildings, so there was very little interest in them. Mingled among them were also hundreds of old, often abandoned, log buildings. A small percentage remained in use, but most were neglected and ignored.

With the restoration of Colonial Williamsburg in the 1920s having caused quite a stir, and a general interest in historic preservation on the rise, there was a significant effort made in the Smokies to save good examples of the "pioneer" architecture. The framed structures were thus removed almost as quickly as their owners vacated the property. The few that do survive are churches, a school, and a few houses that were still in use, or that had potential for administrative use. Unfortunately, framed construction here went back a long way, and some of the framed buildings were older than some of the log ones. The initial sorting out process fostered the erroneous impression that "progress" never made it to the Smokies. The truth is, it did.

In building terminology, the word "frame" refers to a bare skeletal structure that is later filled in, or covered over, with some kind of skin or envelope. "Timberframing" is the oldest of the several framing techniques. Preserved timbers found in peat bogs in Europe date from at least 6,000 years ago. Timberframing makes use of a *small number* of *large timbers*, most of them six inches or more square. The pieces are hewn with a broadax, and the joints of the frame are mortised, tenoned, and pegged together. This method requires the availability of big timbers, and skilled housewrights to make the cuts, angles, and joints, and to put them together properly.

"Balloon framing," the method used in much of today's construction, is attributable largely to George Washington Snow, in Chicago, in 1832. Balloon framing uses a *large number* of *small pieces* of standard-sized 2" × 4" to 2" × 12" sawn lumber. The frame consists of vertical studs, horizontal joists and sloping rafters, all spaced at close intervals, with their joints nailed together. This method requires far smaller individual pieces and less-skilled workmen, but does depend on the availability of sawmills. Otherwise, the material has to be shipped to the site from some distance away. This framing system became popular very quickly in the treeless prairie states, and in 19th century western boomtowns suffering shortages of skilled carpenters. After proving its worth initially in these situations, it eventually caught on everywhere else in the country. In between these extremely heavy and extremely light framing systems, there have been variations on the themes, and mixtures of them.

"Boxed" buildings were a third basic type of "framed" structure found in the Smokies. They represented by far the most hasty and inexpensive kind of construction, yet amazingly, many such buildings stood for long periods, and still do, outside the park. A boxed building actually had no frame, and was literally a large wooden box. The method employed roughsawn lumber about 1 to 1$^1/_2$ inches thick. After the sills and floor joists were set, two boards were nailed together along their edges to form a 90 degree trough. This assembly was stood upright at one corner and nailed to the floor. The process was repeated at each corner, so that there were four "cornerposts." Boards were nailed on edge from the top of one post to the next, providing a headband all around the box. Vertical siding boards nailed at the floor and at the headband formed the walls. Rafters and roofing completed the structure, after which window and door openings were sawn out. Such was the boxed house or outbuilding.

Heavy timberframed structures were extremely rare in the

The L.O. Greenwood boxed house at Smokemont, North Carolina. Boxed houses went up quickly, were cheap to build, and could be added onto easily. *1937 by C.S. Grossman.*

The front porch of the Elijah Oliver house in Cades Cove, Tennessee, was enclosed to serve as a "stranger room." *1975 by Clair Burket.*

℘ Strangers & Kin

Smoky mountain people were legendary for their hospitality. From the earliest accounts of the region, travelers report staying overnight in the homes of residents who had no idea they were coming and charged nothing for a fine supper and a warm bed.

Only in the twentieth century did some farmers build guest houses and cabins and begin charging fees for visitors (mostly fishermen). "Everyone had people acoming fishing, they called it fishers then," said Pearl Caldwell, from Cataloochee. "Everybody's looking for the fishers. And through the summer you had a pretty good job [boarding them]."

Whether they charged for the service or not, mountaineers created little barriers between them and their overnight guests. Some Cades Cove residents framed in their porches for this purpose and called them "stranger rooms" or "Elijah rooms," for the Biblical character. A latch string in the front door of the home, pulled in, locked the family in and the stranger out.

Completely separate buildings were preferred for "long-term strangers" (e.g., sons- and daughters-in-law). On Ellis Monthieth's place in North Carolina, a frame house built behind the main house was called the marriage house: where young people lived until they had enough money to afford a home of their own. In Greenbrier, folks called these second homes honeymoon houses or "weaner" cabins.

The Smokemont church, which still stands near Smokemont Campground, North Carolina, is an example of the use of frame construction in the Smokies. *Circa 1930–35 by Harry Wolf.*

Smokies. Although timberframed houses were built, with the spaces between the timbers filled with bricks or mud-and-sticks, from the earliest colonial days, those methods were not practiced here. The complexity of making the joints, particularly where three or more timbers came together, was so great that the system was justified only where large uninterrupted interior spaces were needed. Therefore, large barns and the workfloors of grist mills were typical cases. The John Cable mill in Cades Cove and several barns in the park are good examples of timberframing.

Balloon framed structures are now limited to a few churches, one school, the Mingus and Reagan mills, and a few houses and outbuildings in Cades Cove and Cataloochee. Except for the mills, which are unpainted, all of the framed structures are recognizable by their horizontal lap siding, exterior paint, and ceiled or paneled interiors.

The sawing of most of the materials was done locally in each case, either by reciprocating sashsaws or circular saws. The sashsaw consisted of a large blade hung inside a wooden frame, or sash, that moved up and down between guides or on a track, like a window sash. The log, on a rolling carriage, passed slowly through the sash, the blade taking about a quarter-inch bite on each downstroke. When the log passed all the way through, it was pulled back, moved over the width of the next board to be cut, and sent back through the saw. Production was low because only small-diameter logs could pass through the sash. The process was slow because the saw was powered by a crank attached to a waterwheel. Even during rainy periods, when there was plenty of water, the sashsaw was very weak compared to the circular saw.

The circular saw was faster and more powerful for two reasons: the blade's motion was rotary, instead of reciprocal; and, it was powered by a steam engine. Small portable steam sawmills began to appear in the mountains in the 1890s. They were wheelmounted, horsedrawn units that could be taken into the woods and fired with slabs and scrap from the very logs that they sawed. Completely self-contained, these little "peckerwood" mills operated on a scale small enough to make it financially feasible for the owner/operator to saw the pattern (all of the sizes and quantities) for one building at a time. Sometimes the job was done on shares. The landowner would give the sawyer half of the total number of logs in order to get enough lumber for his own needs. The sawyer would then sell his half for cash. Many a church, school, store, barn, or house in the Smokies was "sawed out" in this way. After 1900, the advent of commercial logging here provided unlimited lumber products.

The roughsawn exterior siding and interior ceiling, paneling, and flooring for framed houses was often dressed (smoothed) by hand. The interiors of the Becky Cable house,

The Roaring Fork school and church in Tennessee was another example of frame construction. Students of various ages and grade levels learned side by side in the same one-room building. *1928 or '29 by Laura Thornborough.*

the churches in Cades Cove, and the Palmer house, Methodist church, and schoolhouse in Cataloochee all contain handplaned boards. The task of planing is an exhausting one, but not a thankless one. During the tens of thousands of strokes of the razor-sharp plane, the workman feels the bit slice through the wood, sees the thin shavings curl up through the tool and drape over his leading hand, hears that peculiar whistle of the blade, and sniffs the aroma of each fresh slice. As if that were not reward enough, the finished lumber kept on giving. In the raking light of fireplace or setting sun, the shallow ripples on enameled boards make a texture that excites the eye, and mirrors the memory of hard work now over and well done.

Decorative exterior trim on framed houses often answered the fashions of the day. Porch roofs were supported by fancy posts that were chamfered along their edges or turned round on a lathe. Balusters and rails between the posts kept the dogs off the porch and the toddlers on. Lattice gave privacy and partial shade, and served as a windbreak. Flowering vines on the lattice enhanced those functions. On the gables and along the eaves, shingles were applied in various decorative patterns; or, blocks of wood cut in diamond, shamrock, and other shapes, and painted contrasting colors, added a little "gingerbread" look. Except for latheturned posts, all of these decorative elements could be sawn out by hand or shot with a plane, right on the job site. They cost little or nothing, and added much to the appearance of the home.

Paint choices were limited in number, but bright in hue,

☾ Roofs

Many farmers covered their roofs with long, wooden boards over the rafters, according to historian John Morgan. In later years, they replaced the boards with all metal roofs, which added a pleasing *plink-plink* melody to the interior when it rained.

Sometimes, however, a farmer preferred "shakes," long tapered shingles usually made of oak. Seymour Calhoun, who grew up on Hazel Creek, said his grandfather used white pine shingles. He cut down a lot of pines to clear his land, and he didn't want to waste them. They proved a sturdy choice. "We tore the house down 50 years later," Calhoun said, "and that house was still covered with them pine shingles."

Pine or oak, shingle-making was hard work. Store records from Big Creek in the late nineteenth century show one farmer paid his bill for coffee, sugar, and soda with shingles. Through trade, then, everyone in the community could benefit from the skills of a good shingle-maker.

mostly white, red, blue, and yellow. Secondary colors could be mixed from the primary ones. Solid white homes were not the norm, and the framed house without some contrasting trim was rare. One ancient native of Roaring Fork commented that different parts of his home were painted "with every color that Sears & Roebuck had."

Interior trim and finish in framed houses could be of homemade or commercial materials. The aforementioned handplaned panel and ceiling boards were common. Often their edges were beaded with a handplane to dress them up a bit. Commercial material was available in nearby Maryville, Waynesville, Knoxville, and Asheville. The most popular here, as elsewhere, was "beaded ceiling" or "bead board." About 4 to 6 inches wide, its edges were beaded, and a bead ran down the center. The Hiram Caldwell house in Cataloochee today contains the most generous display of this material, which is nailed up in vertical, horizontal, and diagonal patterns.

The frame W.G.B. Messer house in Little Cataloochee, North Carolina had many ornate architectural details. Will Messer was both a master woodcraftsman and blacksmith. *Photo courtesy Beatrice Sisk.*

They appear to be just mere wooden boxes with gabled roofs. They are that, but much more, too. In spite of their simplicity of design, it still required much patience and care spacing studs, joists, and rafters, nailing them properly, and having it all turn out plumb, level, and square. Although they are not now so, neither are many of us.

✿ Lawns & Gardens

Every mountain child remembers "sweeping the yard," a daily chore like washing dishes or feeding the chickens. Many farmers grew broom corn, a stiff variety of sorghum used to make bristles that were tied around a wooden broom handle. Glenn Cardwell, a park ranger with family roots in Greenbrier, said that sweeping the yard not only kept the place neat but kept grass from growing—grass that would attract chiggers and hide snakes. If the grass grew too tall, the children were summoned to mow it with a scythe or graze a closely supervised milk cow in the yard for a short time.

Unlike the neat lawns visible around cabins today, mountain yards usually included a network of trails to the wash place, the woodpile, the kitchen garden, and the smokehouse. "The yards in the Cove were outdoor extensions of the families' living spaces," wrote landscape architect Delce Dyer, who did a historical study of yards in Cades Cove. In addition to "the standard chores," Dyer noted, social gatherings, such as "apple peelings" or "bean stringings" took place in the yard.

Many old photographs of Smoky Mountain homes show grape or wisteria vines cascading across porches or on trellises. On one corner of the yard stood an Eastern red cedar, black walnut, or apple tree. In addition to shade (or nuts and apples, in the case of the latter), the trees provided a safe roost for the ever-present chickens when a hawk or opossum threatened. Poisonous but attractive and

exotic-looking castor beans kept moles from the flower and vegetable beds.

How you decorated your yard reflected in part your family heritage. During the early 19th century, pioneer women wrapped seeds and bulbs in handkerchiefs and carried them

south and west with them when they settled the Smokies. One hundred years later, their granddaughters and great-granddaughters still lined their porches with potted plants and put daffodils and tulips along the front of the house. And today, if you hike a wooded trail during springtime in the Smokies, you may be surprised by a cluster of daffodils, the only trace of the site where a family once lived.

The "Williams boys" on their vine-embellished porch in Gatlinburg, Tennessee. *Circa 1930 by Harry Wolf.*

BARNS & OTHER OUTBUILDINGS

BARNS

A few years ago, an old man stood in a field, in tears, on a cold October night, and watched his barn burn to the ground. A younger relative standing nearby commented softly, "His life's savings were in that barn." The old man did not live long after that. Barns are the soft-spoken heroes of farm buildings. They usually are not taken seriously except by those who use them, or know them for what they are.

If the house was where the living was done, the barn was where the living was made. The barn was the main activity center of the farm, and where the capital equipment of life was

Left to right: the Walker sisters barn had a wagon shed on one side and a livestock pen on the other. The "slip gap" let the hogs or sheep in and out. *1936 by E.E. Exline.* A two-pen drive through barn in Cades Cove,

kept or stored. The draft animals that pulled the wagon and the plow lived there. The cows, whence came the milk, butter, and cheese, lodged there. Chickens, pigs, goats, and sheep, turkeys, guineas, ducks, and geese hung around it. The tools of living— plows, harness, hoes and rakes, harrows, cradles, saws and hames—reposed in the barn. Upstairs in the loft were the winter's fodder and hay. The barn was so critical to a farm operation that it sometimes was built before the house—and its contents were far more valuable than those of the home.

There were many styles of barns in the Smokies. Most of

Tennessee. There was one pen for the cow, another for the mule, and a space for the wagon in between. Upstairs there was plenty of room for fodder and hay. *1958–59 by R.A. Wilhelm.*

them were general purpose structures, as opposed to specialized tobacco, sheep, or milking barns and such. Each farmer built according to his needs, or anticipated needs, no larger, no smaller. The barn had to be adequate in size, but not a waste of timber and labor.

There were several basic barn designs in the Smokies, with variations on each theme. Construction materials consisted of: all log, mixed log and framed, and all framed. Framed, in this sense, refers to heavy timberframing rather than light stud framing. Design and materials are not reliable dating devices because some framed barns were older than some log ones.

The simplest design was very much like the log cabin itself: a rectangular room with a gabled roof. Such a barn could be of

log or framed construction, with only one door large enough to admit a cow, horse, or mule. The interior could be subdivided into stalls with appropriate hayracks, mangers, etc.

Similar to this was the "half-barn," as we might call it, for lack of another name. This type was very common, particularly on the North Carolina side of the Smokies. It consisted of an enclosed stall under one half of the gabled roof, with the other half of the space left open. This arrangement was convenient because it allowed a cow and a horse or mule to be kept in the stall, and the wagon parked in the adjacent open space. Some-

Jim Carr's four-pen crosshall barn provided maximum versatility and looked good while doing it.

times, the half-barn was a story-and-a-half high, with hay
storage space above.

Among the simpler barns was another variation similar to
the halfbarn. However, instead of stall space occupying all of its
half of the roofed area, a small stall stood in one corner and a
separate corncrib in the opposite corner. The two enclosures
were separated by a hall into which a wagon could be backed
to facilitate unloading into the corncrib. The other half of
the roofed area remained open, as with the standard halfbarn.
The sole survivor of this type is at the Ephraim Bales place on
Roaring Fork Motor Nature Trail. Beyond these three types,
barns got bigger and more complicated.

An intermediate-sized design was the two-pen drive-
through barn, which somewhat resembled the dog-trot house.
One of these barns now stands behind the Becky Cable house
in Cades Cove. Two log pens were built about 20 feet apart and
joined by a common roof. This provided a covered hallway in
which to park a wagon or a sled. Access to the loft over either
pen was easy from ladders in the hall or from a wagon bed.

One of the most pleasant styles was the four-pen cross-hall
barn. It was built with one pen at each corner and covered with
a tall gabled roof. The placement of the pens created two halls
that crossed in the center. Inside, this provided a large amount
of stall space, a generous loft for fodder and hay, and the convenience of driveways and entrances from four directions. From
the outside, this style of barn has naturally balanced proportions
and a solid, rooted-to-the ground look. The Noah "Bud" Ogle
barn on Cherokee Orchard Road is a good example of this once-
popular design.

This hickory-
wood latch spring
still works after
about 90 years of
service. You'll find
it in Cataloochee.
*1975 by Dr. Roy
Carroll.*

Another design might be called the "shotgun" barn. It was
similar to the "shotgun" house in that its main body was long
and narrow, and one could look all the way through from one
end to the other. Such barns had several stalls on each side of
the long hallway, and often had additional sheds on each side.
The Enloe-Floyd barn at the Oconaluftee Mountain Farm
Museum is a splendid example, being 50 feet wide (including
sheds) and 60 feet long. It is only upon looking into the cavern-

ous, empty hayloft of one of these monsters that its vastness becomes apparent. A 2,500 square foot suburban home would fit upstairs in this barn; and re-roofing it requires over 16,000 hand-split shingles. To have enough feed to fill the loft, and to have enough stock to eat the feed, speaks of prosperity.

By far, the darling of barn buffs is the cantilevered style. Attributed to the Swiss by some, Germans by others, its ethnic origin has aroused much debate. One advantage of this construction method was that a large hayloft could be built on top of smaller log cribs below, without having support posts to get in the way of wagons, sleds, and various tasks performed on the ground around the barn. Also, large numbers of livestock can be fed in winter by placing hay on the bare ground under the overhang, even if there is deep snow elsewhere.

Practically all cantilever barns fell into one of two categories: two-pen or four-pen. These groups were further subdivided into ones with overhang on the front and rear only, and those with four-way overhang. Building a large four-pen barn with

A "motel" for livestock, this drover's barn at the Mountain Farm Museum furnished food and shelter for pigs, cattle, and horses being driven from the mountains to market. *1955 by Henry Lix.*

overhang all around was a major and complicated undertaking that required plenty of help.

Getting two pens aligned and level with each other was a necessity, and very difficult if the site was on a slope or uneven ground. Building four pens multiplied the chances that something wouldn't turn out just right. Assuming all went well with the pens, the hayloft framing was begun. It rested on the huge cantilever beams that were laid across the tops of the cribs, in one direction only for front and rear overhang, and at right angles to each other for four-way overhang. The bottom surface of each overhanging beam was hewn so that it tapered toward the tip. This was done to reduce the beam's own weight so that it would not sag at the tip. The cantilever principle is a simple one, regardless of how and to what it is applied. The end of any beam that sticks out over a support can hold up some weight as long as there is an equal or greater weight holding down the other end. If both ends of the same beam project over the opposite walls of a building, and the weight on each end is about the same, then all is in equilibrium, as with a balanced seesaw.

To demonstrate this principle to yourself, spread your arms and hands out to your sides at shoulder level, palms up. Notice that everything tapers, from upper arm to forearm, to flat hands to fingertips. Your arms are cantilever beams "resting" on your torso. Have someone place a five-pound bag of flour on one palm and notice that your body tends to lean. Have another bag of flour placed on your other palm, and notice that the load on your body has equalized or balanced. That is the secret of the cantilever beam structural system.

The loft framing was of the ancient timberframed variety, that dates at least from the Middle Ages in Europe and Britain, and employs heavy hewn timbers that are mortised, tenoned, and pegged together. Such framing required considerable skill to lay out and make the cuts and angles. Fitting the pieces together and pegging them into place, while working about three stories in the air, called for steady nerves. Once the framing was finished, it was a relatively straightforward job, albeit an arduous one, to lay the rafters, lath, and shingles.

two-pen drive-through barn

shotgun barn

two-pen cantilever barn

four-pen cantilever barn

In and near the Smokies, the overwhelming majority of cantilever barns were found on the Tennessee side of the state line. A very few appeared on the North Carolina side. There is no known explanation for this. The environment is essentially the same on both sides, as were the skills, inventories, and ethnic backgrounds of the people. Many people on opposing sides of the crest were even related by blood. Thus, the spatial distribution of this barn type is likely to remain one of those minor unsolved mysteries of the universe. Whatever its origins, the cantilever barn is a favorite today. It appears on postcards, placemats, calendars, and in the paintings of many local artists. As well it should. With its high-flying loft, perched on airy-looking cribs, it is a handsome thing.

This replica of a cantilever barn was built in about 1960 by local craftsmen who did much of the preservation work in those days. It has all of the grace, beauty, and strength of the originals.

BLACKSMITH SHOPS

The blacksmith was one of the most important people in any community. Contrary to popular belief, the smith did far, far more than just shoe horses. A basic fact of life was that tools for living had to be made. Then they wore out or broke. The broken scythe mowed no hay. The broken link ruined the whole chain. The blacksmith took care of all of those little technical difficulties suffered by the rest of the population. Most local smiths, like the grist millers, were not full-time professionals. They farmed, and sold their skills on the side. Consequently, their meager shops and equipment betrayed this part-time approach to the trade. As in any business, location was important, so most black-smith shops were right beside the road. After all, there was no point in carrying or hauling heavy iron objects any farther than necessary.

Blacksmith shop buildings were very straightforward and functional. They consisted of four log walls, an earth floor, no windows, and one door. Chinks were usually left open, to let light in and smoke out. The size of the building varied with the size of the smith's trade, 12′ × 14′ to 14′ × 16′ being about average out in the rural areas. This would allow space for tools and iron stock, and swing room for large work.

Internal arrangement of the shop was an extremely per-sonal matter. It depended on whether the man was short or tall, or whether he was left-handed or right. The anvil face was

The Milas Messer blacksmith shop on Cove Creek in Haywood County, North Carolina. Besides black-smithing, Messer tanned leather, made tubs and barrels, and farmed. *1937 by E.E. Exline.*

∽ The Village Blacksmith

Not every farm in the Great Smoky Mountains had a blacksmith shop, but until the 1920s, every *community* could claim at least one. Within each valley, a skilled farmer would sharpen and repair tools, plows, and mattocks for his neighbors in exchange for goods and services. A good blacksmith also could build wagons with the help of a crew and was said to make a wagon "cluck."

Alie Newman Maples, who spent her childhood in the Sugarlands, remembered her grandfather, the village blacksmith. "He was what you call a small man, not more than five feet tall," she said. "He would get out and do all the things you think a big man would do: farm the land and plow." But in his blacksmith shop, she recalled his great presence as a well-respected craftsman.

"I'll always remember some of the tools," she said. "He'd push [the iron] in the coals 'til it got real red hot, then he'd carry it to the anvil and beat it until it got so sharp. Then he'd dump it in a bucket and all that steam just filling that blacksmith shop."

The part of the process Maples liked best, however, was when he stoked the fire. "I was just small and he would say 'c'mon babe, go puff the bellows for me,'" she said. And then Maples would swing her small frame onto the handle of "the puffing box," and the forced air would make the fire burn quickly down to hot coals.

Smoky Mountain blacksmiths preferred to make fires of coal or charcoal made from hickory, a very hard wood that was readily available and burned hot. As more work was done for cash, coal from other parts of Tennessee could be purchased.

Blacksmiths also performed the important task of shoeing horses and mules. According to a former Cullowhee, North Carolina, resident, Clifford Casey, horseshoe iron came straight and the blacksmith had to "put the caulks on." The shoes were then "fitted hot," so that they would burn the hoof to fit irregularities in the iron. Because the hoof contains no nerve endings, Casey said the "hot-fitted" horse didn't feel a thing.

Today, few working hardware blacksmiths remain. Their closest occupational relative is probably the farrier. Farriers, who only shoe horses and mules, no longer "hot-fit" shoes and have to travel great distances to many farms to make a full-time living. John Wright, a Gatlinburg resident who started shoeing horses for the lumber companies during the 1920s, ended up working for some of the riding stables in the park. He told the *Sevier County News* in 1972 that he enjoyed his work, but "there are not many blacksmiths any more and watching me shoe a horse is a novelty to the many visitors in the park."

usually at knuckle height, with the fingers around the hammer handle and the arm straight at the side. And so on. All of these personal particulars meant that the shop really was suited to one person only. However, the general inventory was almost universal in small country shops. Certain constants were there: anvil, leg vise, forge, bellows or crank blower, quench tub, and workbench. Beyond that, hammers, tongs, files, punches, fullers, flatters, and other tools were immensely varied. Outside the shop was the inevitable scrap metal pile, usually including a large number of worn down wagonwheel tires. Bits of scrap, particularly the iron tires, could be turned into many tools and useful objects, from door hinges to bear traps.

The surviving work of most smiths in the Smokies speaks loudly of its "sideline" nature. It was functionally acceptable and aesthetically nondescript, but it worked well enough to hold the community together and keep it going.

Horse and mule shoes crafted into hinges for the root cellar door on the Joe Caughron log house in Cades Cove, Tennessee. *1937 by C.S. Grossman.*

CHICKEN HOUSES

Why did chickens live in houses? A few years ago, a park employee arrived at work one morning at the Becky Cable house in Cades Cove. Back at the barn, she found that a most unbelievable slaughter had occurred. The array of blood, guts, feathers, claws and other miscellaneous chicken parts flung about the ground was truly astounding. Somehow, the gate to the chicken yard had been left open the night before. A fox or weasel got in. No one was ever certain about the number of birds that met their doom, but an even dozen would be close. To a newcomer in chicken husbandry, such a lesson usually "takes" the first time.

Chickens were part of every farm scene. Turkeys, guineas, ducks, geese, and even peafowl were all raised here and there. But the common chicken, *Gallus gallus*, was the universal yard-bird. Of course, some people had more than others; and some took better care of them than others. The really low maintenance way of raising chickens was to let them roost at night in a nearby tree, and feed them table scraps and things by day. That gave real meaning to "scratching for a living." A little more conscientious owner would spike some wooden boxes or short sections of hollow log to the side of his house, about five feet off the ground. The chimney corner was a good place for these. It was warm, sheltered and generally safe from predators. The house at the Oconaluftee Mountain Farm Museum has a few of these.

Those who were really serious about chicken raising, and who had lots of them, usually tried to keep them under control so as to be able to collect them and their eggs in one convenient place. Clipping their wings (feathers only) was a traditional

Left: the Caleb Bales chicken house on Roaring Fork Creek in Tennessee. Note the nests on the outside of the house and the cross braces to prevent the building from being tipped over by bears. *1935 by C.S. Grossman.*

method of keeping them under control. It didn't hurt them anymore than clipping one's fingernails. However, once grounded, they were defenseless against predators and chicken houses became a necessity.

The average log chicken house was about six rounds high, seldom taller than a man's shoulders. They ranged from about 2′ × 6′ to 8′ × 10′ in area. A shed roof was typical, but gabled roofs were also used. Nearly all of them were built of hewn or split logs, which gave flat faces inside and out on which to nail battens. Rubble stone fill under the sills further tightened the

A chicken house on the Chandler Jenkins place near Cosby, Tennessee. The building now stands at the Oconaluftee Mountain Farm Museum. *1937 by E.E. Exline.*

building against predators. Several features on specimens in the Smokies are noteworthy. The Caleb Bales chicken house was so tall and skinny that he nailed bracing poles to it to keep bears from turning it over. The doorway was very small, and Bales locked the chickens up every night. Unable to get himself through the door, Bales built laying nests on the outside of the structure so that the eggs would be more accessible. The Willis Baxter chicken house had a man-sized door, but also featured a small hatch above it. That arrangement allowed the birds to come and go at will via a ladder; yet no predators could get to them with the main door shut. The Baxter chicken house was also a good example of economy of materials and labor. The wall logs were matched, meaning they were split in half lengthwise, each half going into opposite walls.

So what did people do with all those chickens and eggs? They ate a lot of them. However, they also used them for barter at the local store. Chickens and eggs were almost as good as cash for odds and ends like needles and thread, and many a store had a chicken coup standing outside just for holding "trade-ins."

PIG PENS

The pig pen was an element of most mountain farms, since pork was the main meat eaten here. Ecologically, this made sense. For most of the year the swine ran loose, ranging the woods near the house, and doing very well on roots, grubworms, acorns, chestnuts, and

❧ Chicken Thieves

Almost everyone who lived in the country kept chickens. And they weren't the plain white chickens seen in factory farms today. Colorful Plymouth Rocks, Domineckers, Buff Orphingtons, Cochins, and Rhode Island Reds pecked about the yards. Mountain women usually took charge of the chickens and traded the eggs in the local store for shoes and clothing.

Mark Hannah, who grew up in Little Cataloochee, remembered a story about his Aunt Emma Valentine, who heard her chickens squalling and cackling one night. Her husband wasn't home, so she went out to see what "varmint" was invading her chicken house. "Lo and behold," Hannah recalled, "it was two men climbing down the wall with two of her chickens."

Unarmed, Aunt Emma could still be an imposing character, and the men were caught. "You climb right back up there and get two more," she said.

The stunned men complied "they were too scared not to obey her command," Hannah said. "And she told them to go and not come back anymore at night. If they had to have another one—to ask for it—she would give them one."

the like. Thus the farmer had to pay the pig no mind, and there was little labor or expense in feeding him. Ownership of these free-ranging animals was documented by "earmarks" which were various combinations of slits, notches, and holes cut and punched into the creatures' ears when they were young. To keep the animals from ranging too far and getting too wild, hogs were

Chicken nests on the house kept the birds high and dry and away from dogs, cats, weasels, and other fearsome things. *1937 by C.S. Grossman.*

usually fed a ration of corn at regular intervals near the house. Some people blew a horn to call them up. Hog calling by voice, now a competitive event at various Old Timers' Day celebrations, was once an everyday practical skill. In the fall of the year, one or more pigs would be captured and brought to the pig pen, or pig house, to be more precise.

The Walker sisters pig pen in Little Greenbrier, Tennessee. Pigs were fed through the trough in the foreground. *1936 by E.E. Exline.*

The pig pen was a mere container that limited the animal's exercise and protected it from bears. Thus, pig pens were invariably small, 3′ × 6′ to 6′ × 6′ being the norm. Some were so narrow the animal could not even turn around. This was by design. Entry into the pen was a one-way trip for the pig. There he was "topped off," or fattened for a while on corn or chestnuts. Limiting his movement hastened weight gain. One farmer in Cades Cove remarked that he fattened his hogs "till their eyes swole shut and they couldn't stand up." When time for slaughter came, he couldn't fit through the door, even if the pen had one. He was thus killed on the spot, the roof lifted off, and the carcass hauled out.

The pen was a structure only in the loosest sense of the word. Materials were poor, and workmanship was irrelevant. Given its limited and brief function, that was understandable. Most of them consisted of three to five rounds of split rails or logs, crudely notched enough to keep them in place. Various braces were sometimes added to keep the crib from being kicked apart, since a four-hundred pound hog has considerable influence. Nearly all of the pig pens here had heavy puncheon floors, which kept the animal from rooting out. Logs and planks were placed on top and weighted with heavy stones to keep the bears out.

This served long enough to answer the squealing alarm of a threatened hog with rifle fire. However, come a good crisp autumn day, his time was up anyway.

∾ To Catch a Pig

No doubt about it, hogs preferred running free to standing in a pen. Maybe they even knew that being penned meant one of two things—ear notching for identification or fattening for slaughter. Whatever the reason, hogs were often very hard to catch.

Eldridge Caldwell, who grew up in Cataloochee, remembered as a young boy trying to pen several 200-pound hogs. "I got up a bunch a boys there to go with me; there's four of us. And we had a bunch of bear dogs," he recalled. The group set out after the hogs, who took refuge near Polls Gap. Eventually, Caldwell's dogs cornered one hog in a sink hole. When he moved to throw a rope around the hog's neck, however, both he and the animals were attacked by a swarm of yellow jacket wasps. The hog was so mad that it ran after Caldwell. "I'd let him get set for me, and I'd step aside, and he'd run on by me. He follered me, that way." It wasn't the easiest way to catch a hog, but the pair made it back to the farm in record time.

The only way to catch a hog, according to Mark Hannah, was to put a trail of corn up to the pen. Hannah, another Cataloochee native, recalled catching a sow in the pen, securing the door, and then leaving small holes open on the sides. "Later we would return to the pen and find pigs in there with their mother. We would close the holes in the pen and have them caught ready to mark their ears."

PRESERVING THE HARVEST

For most Americans, food preservation was a significant part of domestic work until recent years. In the Smokies, planting, making, and keeping the harvest long remained a self-contained and very personal operation. Each family took care of itself, and that is reflected in their farm buildings. Different foods required different preservation techniques, and often their own peculiar storage conditions. Some like it warm, others cool; some like it moist, others dry. So, food storage structures took different forms.

ROOT CELLARS AND "TATER HOLES"

Root cellars were widely used over much of the United States in historic times. People have long realized the value of "earth-sheltering," as we call it today. Regardless of what's happening on the surface of the ground, be it extreme heat or cold, only a few feet down the temperature remains a constant 56° F. or so. Whatever food is stored there will not wither from heat; nor will it freeze. Root cellars, however, were not very common in the Smokies. The overriding reason was geological. It is very difficult to dig a full-sized cellar by hand here because of the boulders and bedrock that often lie just beneath the surface. Thus, it is not surprising that only two freestanding root cellars were documented among the hundreds of other kinds of outbuildings.

One was located in Happy Valley, just outside the park. It was completely buried, with only its steeply pitched roof and doorway above ground. The cellar was about eight feet square. The roof, five to six feet tall at the ridge, consisted of two layers of puncheons spiked to a heavy ridgepole. The other one was on Deep Creek, and was built shortly after 1900. It stood on a natural bench just above the floodplain, only a few yards from the creek. Immediately behind the bench a hillside rose sharply. The builder's only choice in this situation was to dig into the steep bank. His cellar was about 8' × 10' in area, six rounds of logs high, with a gable of heavily-chinked logs instead of thin boards. It was only partially sunk into the bank because of the heavy earth loading against the log walls, and the low roofline.

The vast majority of people here simply did not build separate root cellars. Instead, they used the "tater hole," a depression commonly dug just in front of the hearth, under the floor of the cabin. In this sheltered location, it did not have to be dug so deep, was not subject to flooding, and was much more convenient than a separate building. The hole was covered with a hinged hatch in the floor. Potatoes there could be retrieved easily, and baked in the ashes in the adjacent fireplace.

APPLE HOUSES

A winter's supply of potatoes might fit into the tater hole under the floor, but an entire apple crop for home use and the wholesale market was a large proposition. It required special care, and its own building. With its thick stone walls and partial or full earth-sheltering, the Smokies apple house was distinctive, and could hardly be mistaken for any other kind of building. There were several styles here, each in answer to the natural grade of the building site.

One type was an earthen cellar of about 16′ × 20′, fully

The earth-sheltered Conrad apple house in Cataloochee, North Carolina. Earth sheltering protected the apple crop from both excessive heat and freezing. *1935 by E.E. Exline.*

buried to the top of its walls, with only a low wooden superstructure and roof above the ground. The wall logs of the superstructure were notched deeply so that they would lie close together, or even touch, for most of their length. Vertical boards lined the insides of the walls, sealing them against the weather and moderating temperature fluctuations. Access at front and rear was through two small hatches about two feet square. Entry was an acrobatic adventure, but once inside there was room to stand and move about.

Another style of apple house was the semi-buried variety. The stone structure penetrated into the earth bank to the point where the natural grade bisected the side walls diagonally, from upper rear to lower front corners. All of this type had heavy stone walls chinked with mud, two storage levels, and gabled roofs. Most of them carried log superstructures 5 to 6 rounds high.

The final variety of apple house was completely freestanding, with no earth sheltering around any of its walls. This design was dependent solely on the thermal mass of its thick stone walls for temperature moderation. Naturally the least efficient, it was very rare.

Some apple houses had little front porch roofs over the entrance to keep direct sunlight out, if the building had to face south or west. They also sometimes had lattice or picket fence-style gates to fend off pets, livestock, or wild creatures who had a taste for apples. After about 1900, the availability of sawdust from commercial logging and lumbering operations provided

The J.M. Conrad apple house in Cataloochee, North Carolina. The above-ground design was not as thermally efficient as an earth-sheltered one, but it avoided a lot of digging. *1936 by E.E. Exline.*

Cliff Oakley at the door of an apple house at Twin Creeks, Tennessee. With a little luck, the apple crop could be sold by Christmas. If not, the lower floor would hold them until they were. *Circa 1930. Photo courtesy Cliff Oakley.*

❧ Apples

Apples aren't what they used to be, according to old-timers from the Smoky Mountains. Wesley Reagen, whose father cultivated an orchard near Roaring Fork until the 1920s, remembered many varieties of apples that have become rare. Each type held a special eating and keeping quality, he said. Winter Johns, for example, were sour apples that grew ripe late in the fall and could be stored in an applehouse through March. Sweeter apples, such as Limbertwig, did not store as well and so were set in a basket near the door of the applehouse to be eaten first.

Lucinda Ogle remembered that her family preserved apples by spreading them on "Granny's drying rock." Ogle, who grew up in the Noah "Bud" Ogle house now located on Cherokee Orchard Road, described the drying rock as a "whopper rock with a flat top, about 12 by 20 feet." When rain clouds rolled over the mountains, her grandmother would call, "Lucinda, child, run your best and bring the fruit from the drying rock!"

More common than a drying rock was "sulphuring" to preserve apples. The cook peeled and sliced pans of fruit, set the pans in a barrel, and laid a pan of sulphur on top. Igniting the sulphur and quickly covering the barrel with a cloth, she bleached the apples white. A special treat all winter long, sulphured apples could be used to make stack pie, cake, or fried pies.

apple growers with excellent and cheap insulation for storing their products at moderate temperatures.

The geographical occurrence of apple houses in the Smokies was related to economics and environment. A few apple trees were found in almost any farmyard, but commercial orchards were located primarily in the higher, cooler, steeper areas around Cosby and Cataloochee. The rougher terrain and poorer roads meant that apple harvests had to be stored for a while and hauled to market one wagonload at a time. As today, long-term storage facilities were essential. Traces of old orchards can be seen in many places throughout the park. Now over-grown by forest vegetation, their long tree rows and alleys give them away. Winter is the best time to look for them. As for apple houses, the only one remaining was rescued from the reforested farm of Will Messer in Little Cataloochee, and now stands at the Oconaluftee Mountain Farm Museum.

SMOKEHOUSES

Next to preserving grain for bread, preserving meat has been one of man's most intense concerns. From Arctic to Equator many methods have been used over the centuries, including salt-ing, sundrying, smoking, pickling, canning, and freezing. The most com-mon methods used by pioneers in the Smokies were salt curing and smoking. The meat in question was invariably pork because hogs cost virtually nothing to raise,

The Leige Oliver smokehouse in Cades Cove, Ten-nessee. Smoke-houses were rarely more than a few feet from the kitchen so that they were conve-nient to use and easy to guard from predators. *1935 by E.E. Exline.*

the curing process was simple, and one could eat every part of the beast from tongue to tail.

"Hog killing," as it was called, began with the first spell of reliably cold weather, usually around Thanksgiving. This was necessary so that the meat would not spoil during the processing and the curing that followed. It was a family operation that required an adequate number of hands to attend to the many steps and details. The desired number of hogs were killed, cleaned, dressed, and divided into the traditional parts such as hams, shoulders, side meat, etc. The "etc." being the other parts that people like to eat, but don't like to think about.

The smokehouse was the place where most of this was done. Early log smokehouses were usually fairly small, 10 × 10 feet or 10 × 12 feet being common. They usually had a low roof, high enough to stand up under, but not much more. Across the tops of the walls, from side to side, lay long horizontal poles on which pieces of meat were hung to cure after processing. Around the walls inside were waist-high benches or shelves on which salting and other processing was done. The walls were usually chinked to keep the smoke in and pests out. Some had wooden floors; others did not. A good tight wooden floor kept the building secure from domestic and wild animals. In cases of earth-floored buildings, a continuous low row of stone rubble was piled around the outside perimeter. Location of the smokehouse rarely varied. It was only a few steps from the kitchen, for reasons of convenience and security. A marauding bear could carry away a whole ham or side of bacon with ease.

If smoking were done in an earth-floored building, the fire could be built right on the ground, or in a narrow trench that ran from front to rear. In some cases, as at the Walker sisters place, the fire in the trench was extinguished when the job was done, and the floorboards returned to their normal place. In a smokehouse with a non-removable floor, the fire could be built

The progressive Palmers built a frame smokehouse and can house in the 1890s in Cataloochee, North Carolina. The stud walls of the can house were filled with sawdust to keep the glass jars from freezing. *1941 by C.S. Grossman.*

✥ Curing Meat

No matter how small the farm in the Great Smoky Mountains, it almost always included a smokehouse. Preserving adequate meat was considered so important to survival that many farm families shared hogs with those less fortunate in the community so no one went hungry.

"They wouldn't *give* you a pig," remembered Winfred Cagle, who grew up in the Deep Creek community, "but they'd swap with you. [My mother] said she knowed people who'd swap a bundle of firewood for a 75-pound pig. You had to swap something, they couldn't give it to you, it was bad luck."

"When the moon was growing [waxing], it was time to kill hogs," said Cagle. Hog-killing could not take place until after a hard freeze and preferably on a day when the temperature stayed below freezing, he added. Men from neighboring farms worked together, and the women gathered to make a huge noon meal. The next Saturday they proceeded to the next farm, until everyone in the valley had enough meat preserved for winter.

The men hauled wood to the site and built a fire. They placed flint rocks on the fire until they were red hot. Next, they dug a hole for a 50-gallon barrel so that the top of the barrel was flush with the ground. They filled the barrel with water and hot rocks to heat it to "scalding." Another team of men knocked the hogs in the head with a hammer and bled them. Each hog was dipped in the hot water until scalded from end to end. A third team skinned the hogs and cut up the backbones and ribs, salted down the hams, and hung them in the smokehouse. A smoky fire might be used in the closed building later to further cure the meat.

Just as every member of the community had to have enough meat for the winter, every part of the hog was used and

The James Huskey smokehouse at the foot of Snag Mountain, Tennessee. Well-battened against plundering bears, this smokehouse would hold a year's supply of hams and bacon. *1941 by C.S. Grossman.*

A hog takes its last ride on a common utility sled.

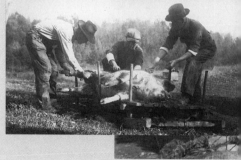

not wasted. The last job of hog-killing day, according to Cagle, was saving the fat from the skin and entrails in large tubs. During the next week, farm women rendered the fat into lard or used it, along with wood ashes from the ash hopper, to make lye soap.

The smokehouse was usually situated close to the main house—not more than 10 feet away. According to Glenn Cardwell, who was born in Greenbrier, it was the "most important building on the farm" and the only one that might have a lock on the door. Dogs kept the bears away, but sometimes it was difficult to keep the dogs away. One spring J. Roy Whaley, also of Greenbrier, noticed some meat missing from the smokehouse. "We got through doing the spring plowing [to find that] someone had left the smokehouse door open, and a dog had carried it out and buried it," Whaley said. "That's the only time we ever had anything stole from us," he added.

in a cast iron kettle or washtub on the floor. The "fires" consisted of oak, hickory, or some other favored wood chips or sawdust, usually green or dampened with water so they would smolder and smoke but not really flare up. Sometimes, the chips were mixed with sand for the same reason.

The objective of the curing process was to preserve the family meat supply so that it could be stored and consumed over a long period. Salt curing was necessary for large pieces such as hams and sides of bacon because only a salt mixture rubbed into the surface would penetrate all the way through the piece ("equalize"), to create a hostile environment for spoiling bacteria.

Smoking could be used for thin bacon-slice strips because the heat of the process dehydrated the meat, depriving bacteria of a moist environment. The chemical effects of smoking also helped to preserve the meat. There are over 300 chemical compounds in wood smoke, the most important ones being the phenols. Phenols kill bacteria on the surface and form an anti-oxidant coating (tar) that retards invasion from the outside. However, the preservative effects of smoking penetrate only about one eighth of an inch, which is why only thin strips can be cured in that way.

The other benefits of smoking meat are flavor and color. One of the quickest ways to start an argument was or is to set two people against each other over whose recipe or technique was better. Another way was to divulge the secrets of an old family recipe. Be that as it may, the smokehouse was found on every farm, and was the answer to a hungry stomach on a cold winter day.

SPRINGHOUSES

When choosing a house site, many criteria came into play, but a good drinking water supply was a prime consideration. Taste, not quantity, was the attribute most desired. There are older people to this day who will not drink city water, and who make regular pilgrimages into the park to fetch water from a favorite spring and take it home. Occasionally, former residents were taken to their old homeplaces in the park in the interest of historical research. Invariably they would bring along jugs to fill at the spring. Coolness, clarity, and reliability were other qualities of a good mountain spring.

The spring was also the mountain refrigerator, so the springhouse was an important building on a hillside farm. Perishable foods, particularly dairy products, were kept inside and cooled by water flowing through the structure. Food was usually placed in heavy crocks capped with ceramic lids, boards, or flat rocks. Canned foods and salted meat were also stored there. Sausage, wrapped in cornshucks, placed in a crock and sealed with fat, would keep through the summer in the springhouse.

Left: cold spring-water, delivered through a wooden trough behind this springhouse, filled another hollow-log trough inside. Food containers in the trough stayed cool; the constant flow of water ran out the spout beside the door.

Since all springhouses were built for the same purpose, most of them were very much alike. Most were small, low structures, 6' × 8', 8' by 10', and 10' × 10' being common sizes. They were just tall enough to stand up in, but some were not even that high. A solid door in the front wall, and sometimes a lattice or picket door, kept wild and domestic animals away from the temptations inside.

The interior layout was a matter of individual taste, somewhat tempered by the lay of the land and location of the spring. Most springhouses were not placed directly over the spring, but a few feet downstream instead. Floors were mere conveniences that provided a dry place to stand and work, although not all

The Palmer springhouse in Cataloochee, North Carolina was fed by 700 feet of hollow log "pipes" from a spring on the hill. *1941 by C.S. Grossman.*

springhouses had them. Heavy puncheons were often used instead of boards, for they would last longer and were not as likely to float away. Better floors of large stone slabs were occasionally used. The spring itself was usually walled up with dry laid stone in order to confine the head, and direct the flow to the building a few feet away.

The terrain immediately around the spring and building site determined the manner in which the flow was handled. On a relatively flat site, the spring flowed through the building in a rock-lined channel and out the other end. (The Walker sisters place has a good example of this.) On a steeper site the water was carried into the building in an elevated trough, which continued through the structure and stopped at the opposite end. (Go to the Elijah Oliver place in Cades Cove to see one of these.) The water exited the trough through a notch in the end, or a hollow wooden spout. Crocks were placed either in the channel in the floor, or in the elevated trough, and were kept cool by the constant flow of water. Sometimes shelves were placed along the side and back walls to provide space for food which did not have to be cooled directly by the water.

Of all farm buildings, the springhouse was perhaps the most delightful place to be in the summer. The location was choice, usually a narrow ravine near the house, shaded by laurel and hemlock and carpeted with fern. On a hot day, it was a good place to linger and drink a dipper of water that was "cold enough to crack your teeth."

CORNCRIBS

Corn was the major food crop in the southern mountains, and it was stored in cribs. Harvesting it was simply a matter of pulling the ears and tossing them onto a wagon driven through the field. Storing it amounted to unloading the wagon into the corncrib, with the shucks still on the ears.

To minimize handling, the wagon was pulled alongside the building. Standing in the wagon, the farmer off-loaded the ears through an opening near the top of the crib. This was usually a hatch in the upper part of the wall; or, as in one crib at the

Oconaluftee Mountain Farm Museum, a portion of the roof was hinged so that it could be propped open. Periodic withdrawals from the crib were made through a much smaller door lower down, usually in the front wall of the crib. Since a bushel or two at a time was all that was needed for a "turn" at the mill, one merely raked down enough from the pile inside for immediate use.

This manner of harvest and storage, simple as it was, determined the design and construction of the crib. Corn had to be dried well before being ground into meal; otherwise, it would gum up the millstones. Thus, all corncribs had certain features in common. They were always built with enough space between the logs to allow plenty of air circulation. They also tended to be as tall and skinny as possible for the same reason. There were limits to its height, lest it topple over. If more capacity were needed, one answer was to build two cribs parallel to each other, with a central hallway for the wagon and a common roof. (This type stands at the Tipton-Oliver place in Cades Cove.)

Sheds were often added to the sides and rear of a corncrib to extend and diversify its usefulness. The wagon might be

A rare cantilevered corn crib in Cades Cove, Tennessee. The farmer could stand in his wagon and load corn through the upper opening. The corn could then be withdrawn in small amounts through the door at the bottom. *1937 by C.S. Grossman.*

parked under one shed, and plows, harrows, and other equipment stored under the other. Thus, the crib became a central core between "plunder" sheds, "plunder" being an old term for miscellaneous stuff. The Walker sisters corncrib was a classic in its day. Today's suburban carport has become the modern equivalent.

After the barn, the corncrib with its sheds could be one of the most versatile of buildings. Its size was to an extent an indicator of the family's wealth. It suggested the number of mouths to be fed in the household, the number of chickens and livestock, the amount of land cultivated, and the quality of the yield. The smallest crib that survives today is at the Ephraim Bales place on Roaring Fork Motor Nature Trail. It is so tiny that you could almost pick it up and hug it. One old-timer said that the land was so rocky and poor there that, "Old Eph prob'ly never even filled that little crib."

Corn in the crib attracted mice and rats, which were controlled by cats or snakes. However, small feisty dogs were also superior at this job, and a good "ratter" was often valued more than a large lazy hound.

The all-time champion "plunder shed." The Walker sisters corn crib with wagon, hames, barbed wire, brooms, firewood, and anything else that was used on the farm. *1936 by C.S. Grossman.*

GRIST MILLS

Many grains were grown in the Smokies, including corn, wheat, oats, barley, and rye. Corn was king, and wheat the queen. All of them were food for man and livestock. Some of them made well-known beverages. In order to store for long periods, grain must be kept hard and dry. The way to convert grain to usable food is to grind or shear it into minute fragments, add water or milk, and cook it into a mush or bread. Grist mills did the grinding and sifting and sorting of grains into the various cereal products.

Mills fell into three categories in terms of output and clientele: commercial, custom, and family. Commercial mills did a large volume of business and usually sold their products in bulk to stores, bakers, or other users on a wholesale scale. Or, they sold goods packaged under their own labels. There were no large commercial mills in what is now the national park. Custom mills did a fairly large business. They sold wholesale, but also "custom ground" their customers' grain to suit individual needs.

The John Cable Mill ground cornmeal, wheat flour, and sawed lumber in a now-missing sawmill shed. *1936 by E.E. Exline.*

❁ At the Mill

Dewey Webb will never forget the sound of the waterwheel when he took his family's grain to McClure's mill. "I was fascinated listening to those wooden cogs going into the wooden spokes. It made a screee-eeeching sound," he said. "No steel cogs about it."

Inside a tub mill, the runner stone turned slowly over a stationary bed stone. Herb Clabo, who lived on Roaring Fork, said the rock turned slowly so that meal wouldn't get burned or develop a smoke taste. It could take four hours to make a single bushel of corn meal. "The miller knew you, and he knew how you wanted your meal," Clabo added. "You're so-and-so's son, you need fine meal."

Lucinda Ogle's grandparents operated a tub mill, so when she was a child her grand-mother sometimes sent her to shut the mill down. Her job was to remove the stick which dropped the gate into the trough which stopped the water from turning the mill wheel. As Ogle left the porch, her grandmother sometimes reminded her not to play in the meal. "But I did!" Ogle admitted. "It was better than playing in the sand pile, to let the meal pour through my little fingers."

Interior view of the Jim Carr tub mill near the Newfound Gap Road, Tennessee.

Private or family mills were small, usually built by the owner, and served his own family; although some helped out the neighbors now and then. Mills in the Smokies fell into the two latter classes.

All of the mills here were powered by running water from nearby streams. However, there were several types of water-powered devices used: vertical waterwheels, horizontal tub wheels, and manufactured, enclosed turbines. The number and variety of functions varied with each mill. The John Cable mill in Cades Cove was powered by an overshot waterwheel. It is what we visualize when we think of traditional "old mills." It could grind corn and wheat, but could not separate wheat products into whole wheat flour, fine white flour, middlings, and bran. The Mingus mill in the Oconaluftee community was powered by two turbines, manufactured by a company that is still in business. Therefore, there is no familiar waterwheel beside the building. However, it was a good-sized custom mill that could shell corn, grind cornmeal, clean wheat, and grind and bolt it into the traditional wheat products. It operated at wholesale and retail levels.

The tiny little tub mills once found all through the Smokies were powered by a horizontal "tub wheel," whose vanes were struck by fast-moving water. They were family-owned, and could grind a small amount of cornmeal or crack a little chicken feed. Two good examples still stand along the Noah "Bud" Ogle Self-guiding Nature Trail and the Roaring Fork Motor Nature Trail.

Taking shelled corn to the small mill on one's own property was not a particularly noteworthy event. Taking one's grain to the local community mill was. The routine was for the miller to remove the customer's grain from his sack, grind it to his liking, and return the product to the same sack. For this service he extracted his toll, which varied from $1/12$ to $1/8$ of the grain. The fun part of this was waiting for your "turn" to be ground. As most mills were only open once a week on "mill day," everyone showed up at once. There was a great deal of pocketknife swapping, horsetrading, bragging, and lying about fish caught and bears killed, as the miller worked himself ragged trying to serve everyone. The miller was usually a farmer like everyone else around him. Yet he had that extra something, his mill, that no community could do without.

GLOSSARY

adze—a tool used to smooth or finish a timber that has already been hewn with a broadax. It is swung in short, careful strokes just ahead of the workman's leading foot, which is why it is sometimes called a "foot adze." Also, the act of smoothing a rough-hewn timber with an adze by removing thin shavings or chips.

auger—a T-shaped tool used to bore holes in timber. Shaped like a giant corkscrew, its bit is twisted into the wood with both hands, using the T-handle.

balloon-framed (stud-framed)—a building system consisting of many small pieces (studs, joists, and rafters), spaced closely together, with their joints nailed. The frame is then covered with exterior siding and a roof.

batten—a thin strip of wood, split or sawn, nailed over the "chinks" in a log wall, or the cracks between the boards in a wall.

board brake—a heavy forked piece of tree crotch in which bolts of wood are braced while being split into shingles with a froe.

bolt—a section of log of the same length as the shingles, palings, or battens to be split from it. Also, the fat wedges of wood split from the section. Also, the act of reducing the log into such shapes and sizes.

broadax—an ax with a very broad head and bit that is used to hew timber from the round log. Its bit is beveled on one side only, and its short handle is curved away from the timber so that the user's knuckles do not scrub on the log.

bust—local term for split or rive. To "bust" firewood, fence rails, shingles, palings, etc., with maul and wedges or froe and club.

cat hole—a small hole 3 or 4 inches square in the bottom of a door or wall so that cats could come and go. The historic version of today's "doggie door."

chalkline—a straight line made on a log or piece of timber with a string impregnated with chalk. The string is stretched tightly along the work, pulled up and let go, "snapping" the chalk onto the wood.

chink—the crack or open space between the logs in a wall.

chinking—the mud and/or wood and other materials placed in the chinks to seal them from the weather.

comb—the ridge of a roof, so-called because the ends of the top row of shingles stick up like the teeth of a comb, or like a rooster's comb.

corner chisel—a large chisel, whose bit is shaped like a piece of angle-iron. The edges of the bit are about $3/4$ to 1 inch long each way, and the tool is used to square up round holes in timber.

corner timbering—same as corner "notching," used mostly in an academic context.

crib—in log building terminology, the log walls only, not including floor or roof. For example, "the crib is ten rounds high."

drawknife—a tool that is drawn along small work such as shingles, chair legs, etc., to shape and smooth the piece. The beveled blade lies at right or acute angles to the work, has a handle at each end, and is drawn toward the user.

exposure—the bottom end of a shingle that is not covered by the one above it, i.e., that portion exposed to the weather. On a good roof, only about one-third was left exposed; the more overlap, the better.

framed—a system of building in which a framework is constructed first, then covered on the outside with an envelope or sheath of weather-proof material. See balloon-framed and timber-framed.

froe—a tool used to split (rive) shingles or palings from a bolt (wedge-shaped chunk of log). It is L-shaped, with an upright wooden handle and a horizontal blade. The back (upper) edge of the blade is struck with a wooden club to drive it into the wood. It is then used to pry the shingle off the bolt, rather than slice it off. The froe is therefore supposed to be relatively dull; hence the expression, "dull as a froe."

froe club—the one-handed wooden club used to strike the froe blade. It is usually made of hickory, persimmon, dogwood, or some other hard, tough wood.

gable—the vertical triangle at each end of a gabled roof, as defined by the roof slopes on either side of it. Gables were closed with various materials: logs, lumber, shingles.

gabled roof—a roof with two slopes, shaped basically like a pup tent.

glut—a large, fat wooden wedge used to split fence rails, firewood, logs, etc. It is driven with a large, two-handed maul into a small crack started by a thin metal wedge. Gluts were made of dogwood, persimmon, or other hard, tough wood.

granny hole—a small window-like hole in the wall of a house, usually next to the fireplace, at which "Granny" could sit and keep an eye on things outside.

heartwood—the center or core of a tree, and usually the hardest wood.

hew—to shape a log into a timber with a broadax, usually into a square or rectangular cross-section.

hew to the line—to hew exactly to a straight chalkline that has been snapped onto a log. "Almost there" is no good.

joist—a timber, or plank on edge, spanning from sill to sill, on which the floor is laid; or spanning the tops of the walls on which the ceiling boards are laid.

latch string—a string of rawhide or twine that hung on the outside of the door of the house, and lifted the latch inside. At night it was usually pulled back inside through its tiny hole for security. The expression, "The latch string is always out," means, "You are always welcome. Come to see us."

lath—long, narrow, thin strips of wood that lie across the upper surface of the rafters, onto which the shingles are nailed.

maul—a large, two-handed wooden club used to drive gluts, fence-posts, etc.

middle wood—the middle layer of wood in a tree, between the heart-wood and sapwood. It is often the best quality for many uses.

mortise (mortice)—a square or rectangular hole in a timber or piece of lumber, into which a matching tenon is fitted, thus joining two or three pieces of wood. The joint thus formed was often drilled and pegged for further strength and stability.

notch—the cut made at the end of a log to lock it to other logs. Notches were made at the corners of a building, and where a partition tied into a wall. Different notches took more or less time and skill to make, and performed better or worse than others, in theory. In reality, all styles seem to have performed about equally well.

paling—a long, thin split board used in fencing. Similar to a picket, but uneven in surface texture and cross-section due to being split instead of sawn.

pen—in log building terminology, the basic 4-sided building unit used to describe the shape and/or size of a structure. For example, a single pen cabin, a four pen barn, etc.

pier—a small post of wood or pile of stone that supports part of a building. Usually, the piers used here were of natural-shaped stones, stacked or laid without mortar (dry laid), or of rot-resistant wood such as locust or cedar.

plate—the topmost timber or log on a wall, on which the bottom ends of the rafters rest.

puncheon—a wide, thick wooden slab used as flooring. Usually, one-half of a split log, dressed smooth on the upper (walking) surface and left half-round on the underside.

purlin—a log or timber that runs from gable to gable along the long axis of a building, to which long shingles or boards are nailed. Purlins were used very early here, to eliminate the need for rafters and lath.

rafters—sloping poles or timbers that rest on top of the walls and hold up the roof.

rive—to split shingles, palings, or battens from a bolt of wood, with a froe and club.

roof boards—local term for wooden shingles.

round—in log construction, one layer (four) of logs in a crib. A building is so many "rounds" high.

sapwood—the outermost layer of wood in a tree, usually softer than the middle wood or heart.

scribe—a tool used to draw or scratch (inscribe) a line on a piece of timber, lumber, or log. The line serves as a guide for cuts with a saw, ax, or chisel. A common type of scribe resembles a drafting compass, and is used in laying out notches on the ends of logs.

shaving horse—a long stool or bench-like device on which a workman sits astride and lays small pieces of work to shave with a drawknife. The work is held down with a foot-operated jaw or head.

shed roof—a tilted roof with only one slope.

sills—the bottommost pair of logs or timbers, on the ground or on piers, on which the rest of the building is built.

slick—a giant chisel with a bit 2–3 inches wide, and a two-handed handle about 2–3 feet long. It is used to smooth or "slick" timber, clean out mortises, cut tenons, etc.

stop the cracks—same as to "chink the walls."

stud—a small, vertical building member, usually about 2 x 4 inches in cross-section, which is used with many more of the same to frame a wall or partition.

tater hole—a hole under the floor of a house or cabin, usually in front of the hearth, where potatoes were stored for the winter. It was reached by lifting a hatch or simply a couple of floorboards.

tenon—a square or rectangular stub on the end of a timber or piece of lumber, which fits into a matching mortise, thus joining two or three pieces together. The joint is usually drilled and pegged for improved strength and stability.

timber-framed—a building system consisting of a heavy framework of a few large timbers (posts, beams, joists, rafters), with their joints mortised and tenoned together. The frame is either covered on the outside with weatherboarding, or the spaces between the posts filled with brick, stone, mud and sticks, or other material.

trenail (trunnel)—literally, a "nail" made from a piece of a tree. Wooden pegs were used to secure a joint between two or more pieces of timber. Large ones, one inch or more in diameter and up to a foot long, were used in the heavy frames of barns, bridges, etc. They were usually cut into hexagonal or octagonal cross-sections (like a pencil), and driven into round holes. The sharp ridges would bite into the walls of the holes and hold better than if round and smooth. Smaller pegs were used in making furniture.

ABOUT THE AUTHOR

Ed Trout was the Park Historian for the Great Smokies from 1975 until his retirement in 1994. Although a general "garden variety" historian, his passion has always been old buildings, tools, and the products of simple technology.